Moments for Grandparents

by Robert Strand

First printing, January 1995
Second printing, January 2006

ISBN: 0-89221-281-0
Library of Congress Catalog Number: 94-69836

Cover design by Left Coast Design, Portland, OR.
Cover illustration by Maureen Scullin.

All Scripture references are from the New International Version, unless otherwise noted.

New Leaf Press
A Division of New Leaf Publishing Group
www.newleafpress.net

Printed in China

Presented to:

Beverly and Bill

Presented by:

Warry and Zed

with love,

Date:

Dec. 24th 2008

Day 1
If You Were Born Before 1945 . . .

We are survivors! Consider some of the changes we have witnessed: We were born before television, penicillin, polio shots, frozen foods, Xerox, plastic, contact lenses, frisbees, the pill, radar, credit cards, split atoms, laser beams, ball-point pens, pantyhose, dishwashers, clothes dryers, electric blankets, air conditioners, drip-dry clothes, computers, and before anybody walked on the moon!

We got married first and then lived together! How quaint!

In our time, closets were for clothes, not for "coming out" of, bunnies were small rabbits, and rabbits were not Volkswagons. Designer jeans were scheming girls named Jean or Jeanne and having a meaningful relationship meant getting along well with our cousins.

We thought fast food was what you ate during Lent, and outer space was the back of the Bijou Theater. We were before house-husbands, gay rights, computer dating, dual careers, day care centers, group therapy, and nursing homes. We never heard of FM radio, CDs, computers, cellular phones, artificial hearts, word processors, yogurt, and guys wearing earrings. For us . . . time-sharing meant togetherness, not computers or condominiums; a "chip" meant a piece of wood; hardware meant screws and nails, and software wasn't even a word!

In 1940, "Made in Japan" meant junk and the term "making out" referred to how you did on your exam. Pizzas, McDonalds, Burger

King, and instant coffee were unheard of. We hit the scene when there were five and dime stores, where you actually bought things for five and ten cents. Snelgrove's or Farr's sold ice cream cones for a nickel or a dime. For one nickel you could ride a streetcar, buy a Coke, or enough stamps to mail one letter and two postcards. You could buy a new Chevy coupe for $600, but who could afford one? A pity, too, because gas was 11 cents a gallon!

In our day grass was mowed, coke was a cold drink, and pot was something you cooked in. Rock music was Grandma's lullaby.

We were certainly not before the difference between the sexes was discovered but we were surely before the sex change; we had to make do with what we had. And, we were the last generation that was so dumb as to think you needed a husband to have a baby!

No wonder we are so confused and that there is such a generation gap today.

BUT WE SURVIVED!!!!

WHAT BETTER REASON TO CELEBRATE?

Today's Quote: *When a man falls into his anecdotage, it is a sign for him to retire.* — Benjamin Disraeli

Today's Verse: You have made my days a mere handbreadth; the span of my years is as nothing before you. Each man's life is but a breath (Ps. 39:5).

Day 2
I'm Tired

Don't know about you . . . but as for me, I'm tired! For many years I've been blaming it on middle age, old age, or just plain aging, iron poor blood, lack of vitamins, air pollution, saccharin, obesity, dieting, underarm odor, dandruff, plaque on my teeth, lower back pain, greying hair, and a dozen or more other problems that really make you wonder if life is worth living after all.

But I've just found out, tain't that at all! I'm tired because I'm overworked, I've found out that there are just too few people working, so it's because of overwork!

Consider that the population of our country is about 250 million and about 114 million are retired. That leaves about 136 million to do the work. There are 95 million in school which leaves 41 million to do the work. Of this total there are 22 million employed by the government. That leaves only about 19 million to do the work!

Of this total 4 million are in the armed forces of the U.S. This leaves us only about a remaining 15 million to do the work! Now subtract from that total the 14.8 million who work for the state, city, and county governments and that leaves only 200,000 to do the work!

We must not forget that our country has 188,000 people at any one time in hospitals so we now have only 12,000 people left to do any work!

On most days, there are about 11,998 people serving time in our prisons! Subtract that total and that leaves only TWO people to do the work! And it looks like it's YOU and ME! And you're sitting down to read this! That leaves only ME . . . no wonder I'm tired!

And isn't it fun to play games with numbers and nonsense. The bottom line is that work is a very important part of life and living! We're of the generation which had a strong work ethic. We were told, and have found it to be true, that God helps those who help themselves. We've created a world of wealth by jobs and hard work and creativity and perseverance and the entreprenuerial spirit! But have we done a good job in passing along these principles to the next two or three generations who are following us?

Today's Quote: *By working faithfully eight hours a day, you may eventually get to be a boss and work twelve hours a day.* — Robert Frost

Today's Verse: Whatever you do, work at it with all your heart, as working for the Lord, not for men (Col. 3:23).

Day 3
My Get Up and Go . . .

How do I know that my youth's all spent?
Well, my get up and go has got up and went.
But in spite of it all, I am able to grin
When I recall where my get up has been.
Old age is golden, so I've heard it said,
But sometimes I wonder, when I get into bed.
My ears in a drawer and teeth in a cup,
My eyes on the table until I wake up.
The sleep dims my eyes, I say to myself . . .
"Is there anything else I should lay on the shelf?"

And I am happy to say as I close my door,
My friends are the same, perhaps even more.
When I was young, my slippers were red,
I could kick up my heels right over my head,
When I grew older my slippers were blue,
But still I could dance the whole night through.
Now I am old, my slippers are black.
I walk to the store and puff my way back;
The reason I know my youth is all spent,
My get up and go has got up and went!

But I really don't mind,
When I think with a grin
Of all the grand places my get up has been.
Since I have retired from life's competition,
I busy myself with complete repetition.
I get up each morning, dust off my wits,
Pick up my paper, and read the "Obits,"
If my name is missing,
I know I'm not dead.
SO I EAT A GOOD BREAKFAST AND GO BACK TO BED!*

*Rose Hodgin, *Parables, Etc.*, May 1992.

Today's Quote: *I consider that the old have gone before us along a road which we must all travel in our turn and it is good we should ask them of the nature of that road, whether it be rough and difficult or easy and smooth.* — Plato

Today's Verse: Praise be to the Lord, who this day has not left you without a kinsman-redeemer. May he become famous throughout Israel! He will renew your life and sustain you in your old age" (Ruth 4:14–15).

Day 4
What Do You See When You Look at Me?

The following was written for her caregivers by a woman in a geriatric ward in an English hospital:

What do you see? Are you thinking when you look at me . . .
A crabbed old woman, not very wise,
Uncertain of habit with faraway eyes,
Who dribbles her food and makes no reply,
When you say in a loud voice . . . "I do wish you'd try."
Is that what you're thinking, is that what you see?
Then open your eyes, you're not looking at me.
I'll tell you who I am as I sit here so still,
As I move at your bidding, eat at your will.
I'm a small child of 10 with a father and mother,
Brothers and sisters who love.
A young girl of 16 with wings on her feet
Dreaming that soon a love she will meet.
A bride at 20, my heart gives a leap,
Remembering vows I promised to keep.
At 25 now, I have young of my own
Who need me to build a happy home.
A woman of 30, my young now grown fast,
Bound together with ties that should last.

At 40, my young sons have grown up,
My man's beside me to see I don't mourn.
At 50 once more babies play around my knee.
Again we know children, my loved one and me.
Dark days are upon me, my husband is dead.
I look at the future, I shudder with dread.
For my young are all rearing young of their own,
And I think of the years and the love that I've known.
I'm an old woman now and nature is cruel.
'Tis her jest to make old age look like a fool.
The body it crumbles, grace and vigor depart.
There is stone where I once had a heart.
But inside this old carcass a young girl still dwells,
Now again my bittered heart swells.
I remember the joys, I remember the pain
And I'm loving and living life over again.
I think of the years, all too few, gone too fast,
And accept the fact that nothing lasts.
So open your eyes, open and see, not a crabbed old woman,
Look closer . . . see ME!

Today's Quote: *My diseases are an asthma and a dropsy and, what is less curable, seventy-five.* — Dr. Samuel Johnson

Today's Verse: Cast all your anxiety on Him because He cares for you (1 Pet. 5:7).

Day 5
Insurance Policy

During the middle of the "Great Depression" of the 1930s, we hear of the story of one poverty-stricken older woman. Times have been tough, life has become grim. Many widows were struggling for their meager meals.

One day this older woman, dressed very poorly, but neat and clean, timidly approached the front desk of an insurance office in Minneapolis, Minnesota. She asked if it would be possible for her to stop making payments on the yellowed policy clutched in her farm-weathered, work-worn fingers. Then she offered it to the clerk for a look.

The clerk gave it a quick, perfunctory glance, opened it, and studied it with intense amazement. "This is quite valuable," he said. "Yes, I would advise you to stop paying the premiums now, after all these years. Have you talked with your husband about this?"

"No," she said, looking down, "He's been dead three years, now."

"What!?" exclaimed the clerk. "But this is a policy on his life!"

She looked at him and said, "Please, I don't understand."

Carefully this time, he looked at her and replied, "Madam, this is a life insurance policy on his life in the amount of $300,000. This should have been paid to you upon his death."

Then he paused, "Please have a seat, I'll be right back." He took his leave with policy in hand and went for a supervisor. They both soon appeared, "Would you come with us?" They took her into one of the offices and explained to her again.

Soon, they had figured out the benefit of $300,000 which was to be paid to her plus the three years of overpaid premiums with the accumulated interest on those payments. She left that office with a very generous check in hand. And walked as though the burdens of life had been lifted from her shoulders!

She was able to begin experiencing the financial security which had been hers all the time but had not been known to her! Can you imagine the sense of relief? Perhaps the impact of the money in her life was unknown until she stopped by her bank. What a happy day!

Is there a parallel in your life? When the decision has been made to become part of the kingdom of God, are you realizing all that you may have as benefits and blessings? Are you living beneath your privileges? We are all looking for security in life which can only be ours when we commit our living into God's hands. Security is not in the absence of danger or in having a large bank account, but in the presence of God!

Today's Quote: *God is as great in minuteness as He is in magnitude.*

Today's Verse: Now all has been heard; here is the conclusion of the matter: Fear God and keep His commandments, for this is the whole duty of man (Eccles. 12:13).

Day 6
Oldest Living Things

A careful study of tree rings in California's 4,000-year-old bristlecone pine trees has led scientists to modify the radio-carbon dating of artifacts which has been used since 1949. These trees are the oldest known living things on the face of the earth.

This discovery is also causing a re-writing of histories which have credited Egypt and the Middle East as the source of Europe's advance from barbarism to civilization. Scientifically corrected timetables now show that many of Europe's earliest tombs, monuments, temples, and tools actually predate or are older than their counterparts in the Middle East.

For instance, chamber tombs in Brittany are now being dated 1,500 years older than the pyramids of Egypt! And it is the temples of Malta, not Mesopotamia, which must now be seen as the world's oldest free-standing stone monuments. So we are discovering that it may be later than we thought!

It's a strong possibility that we have misjudged the ancients of the European area. In the past it was thought that civilization and the advances from the Stone Age came from the Middle East and influenced the peoples of the European continent. Current discoveries are causing a re-thinking about this advance. It may well have been the other way around!

Don't such things absolutely fascinate you? I find within me an insatiable desire to learn about our past, as well as to take a look into the future.

We're really talking about time and how it's been measured. Speaking about time, did you hear about the little boy who was allowed to stay up well beyond his normal bedtime because his grandparents were visiting? The clock struck 11:00 and he listened in rapt attention, counting each strike. When the grandfather clock had finished chiming he spoke up and said, "It's later than it's ever been before."

It's so easy to get that sense in our present-day world. Times are changing, events are moving rapidly to some kind of a climax, folks are worried about issues that have not been problems before, and there's a sense of the urgent upon us.

As a person, you are older than you have ever been! This world is older than it's been. We are all aging, and we are all moving to a conclusion. Have you given any thought to your own conclusion? What of your day of dying? Have you taken care of your eternal destiny?

Today's Quote: *We have to live but one day at a time, but we are living for eternity in that one day!* — Anonymous

Today's Verse: I have been young, and now am old; yet have I not seen the righteous forsaken, nor his seed begging bread (Ps. 37:25;KJV).

Day 7
Why Do You Do That?

Josh looked up from his super-hero action figure and watched his grandmother ease out of her chair. There she went — so slowly and unobtrusively that not a soul would notice.

Not a soul but Josh. He continued to watch her curiously as she picked up his shoes from the middle of the floor and put them where they belonged, near the back door.

"Grandma," he called out casually, "why do you do that?"

"Do what, dear?" his grandmother asked as she stepped gently away from the door.

"You know . . . make those noises. Grandma Jean doesn't make noises when she stands up or sits down, and she digs in the garden and helps Grandpa with his chores and everything. But you make noises all the time, Grandma."

This dignified lady who had just been told she "made noises" worked very hard not to betray the smile hidden behind her lips as she faced Observant Josh.

"Can you tell me what kind of noises I make?"

"Oh sure," the tyke said as he took her place in the comfortable chair. He placed his hands on each armrest, furrowed his brow, and with a theatrical flourish that would make an Academy Award-winner proud, began his best impersonation.

"Ohhhh…mmhh. Oh, my…." The moaning and groaning became so exaggerated, Grandma was sure he was milking the performance for all it was worth. She stopped him and attempted to look stern.

"Now Joshua, surely it's not like that."

He thought for a minute. "No, Grandma . . . it's not. Usually, it's much worse!"

Oh, boy! Can our grandkids ever know how much truth they make us endure?

I'm not sure what life-changing lesson this little story serves us with, except, in everything we do, let's make sure we enjoy these wonderful gifts from God. Our Heavenly Father has entrusted these little charges to us and we never know when they're watching and observing us, so let's make sure our grandchildren see Christ in us.

Grandchildren. They're totally unique!

Today's Quote: *Few things are harder to put up with than the annoyance of a good example.* — Samuel Langhorne Clemens (better known as Mark Twain)

Today's Verse: Children's children are the crown of old men . . ." (Prov. 17:6).

Day 8
Thee Onederful Werld ov Wirds

I take it you already know of tough and bough and cough and dough.

Others may stumble, but not you, on hiccough, thorough, lough, and through.

Beware of heard, a dreadful word. That looks like beard and sounds like bird.

And dead . . . it's said like bed, not bead. For goodness sake, don't call it deed.

Watch out for meat and great and threat: they rhyme with suite and straight and debt.

A moth is not a moth in mother, nor both in bother, broth in brother.

And here is not a match for there, nor dear and fear and pear and bear.

And then there's dose and rose and lose . . . just look them up . . . and goose and choose, and cork and work, and card and ward, and font and front, and word and sword, and do and go, then thwart and cart. Come, come I've hardly made a start.

There's also click and clique, and grove and glove, and hope and soap, and move and love; there's sane and seine, and soup and soul, there's lean and lien, and fowl and bowl.

How about pear and pair and pare? There is also fear and fair and fare.

A dreadful language? Man alive . . . I'd mastered it when I was five!*

Language . . . how wonderful it is. It's how we communicate with each other. And being a grandparent hasn't made it any easier when attempting to talk with our grandkids. We find that they are into information highways, Reeboks, CDs, roms, and rap. Many of the solid, foundational words which we grew up with are long gone from today's younger vocabulary. Just say some of the following words . . . they mean two different things to two different generations: square, gay, politically correct, grass, rock music, software, hardware, time-sharing, chip, and low-rider.

Some things are still basic, foundational . . . such as love. It's understood in any language when the actions are seen. Maybe, a grandparent is the only person available to that young life who has the patience and time to make the effort to listen, to communicate. Perhaps you may be the only one who can instill life principles into young heads. It's more than just talking . . . it's communicating, it's caring, it's loving, it's spending time, it's listening creatively, it's being available!

*Gene Sikkink, *Parables, Etc.*, 11/91.

Today's Quote: *Slang is language that takes off its coat, spits on its hands, and goes to work.* — Carl Sandburg

Today's Verse: The Spirit gives life; the flesh counts for nothing. The words I have spoken to you are spirit and they are life (John 6:63).

Day 9
Age Discrimination

Warren Buffet of Omaha, Nebraska, made the cover story in *Fortune* magazine a few years ago. It's the story of one of our country's most successful billionaires. Warren Buffet has been an enormous success in investing in all kinds of companies as he has built up the holdings of his conglomerate, Berkshire Hathaway. He's been called "The Wizard of Omaha" and looks for strong companies well-positioned in their markets. He is famous for taking over companies and leaving the current management in place rather than replacing them.

Now, here's our point of interest. One of his companies is the Nebraska Furniture Mart, founded by Rose Blumkin. Following is *Fortune's* description of Buffet's dealings with the Blumkins:

> With the family Buffet usually refers to as "the amazing Blumkins," who run the Nebraska Furniture Mart, the drill is dinner, held every few weeks at an Omaha restaurant. The Blumkins attending usually include Louis, 68, and his sons, Rom, 39; Irv, 35; and Steve, 33.
>
> The matriarch of the family and chairman of the Furniture Mart is Rose Blumkin, who emigrated from Russia as a young woman, started a tiny furniture store that offered rock bottom prices . . . her motto is "Sell cheap and tell the truth" . . . and built it into a business that last year did $140 million

in sales. At age 94, she still works seven days a week in the carpet department. Buffet says in his new annual report that she is clearly gathering speed and "may well reach her full potential in another five or ten years. Therefore, I've persuaded the Board to scrap our mandatory-retirement-at-100 policy." It's about time, he adds: "With every passing year, this policy has seemed sillier to me."

He jests, true, but Buffet simply does not regard age as having any bearing on how able a manager is. Perhaps because he has tended to buy good managements and stick with them, he has worked over the years with an unusually large number of older executives and treasured their abilities. . . . He says, "Good managers are so scarce I can't afford the luxury of letting them go just because they've added a year to their age."*

Now, I understand, that Rose Blumkin decided to retire . . . but that didn't work, so she has now started her own carpet company, separate from the Nebraska Furniture Mart, so she can manage it as she sees fit!

*Fortune, 4/11/88, page 88.

Today's Quote: *Every generation laughs at the old fashions, but follows religiously the new.* — Henry David Thoreau

Today's Verse: I was young and now I am old, yet I have never seen the righteous forsaken or their children begging bread (Ps. 37:25).

Day 10
Enthusiastic Teaching

Howard Hendricks tells of an 83-year-old woman that he and some other conference leaders had lunch with during a Sunday school convention in Chicago. In the course of conversation it was learned that she was a teacher of 13 junior high boys in a church of 55 attendees. She was asked why she was attending the conference.

"I'm on a pension . . . my husband died years ago," she replied, "and, frankly, this is the first time a convention has come close enough to my home so I could afford to attend. I bought a bus ticket and rode all night to get here this morning and attend two workshops. I want to learn something that will make me a better teacher."

Three convention speakers slithered across the ground back to the convention after that encounter. I couldn't help thinking about all the frauds across America who would be breaking their arms patting themselves on the back if they had 13 boys in a Sunday school of 55 church-goers. "Who, me go to a Sunday school convention? Man, I can tell them how to do it!" Not this woman.

You know, she tipped her hand . . . she told us she had a passion to communicate! I heard a sequel to this story some time later. A doctor told me there are 84 young men in or moving toward the Christian ministry as a result of this woman's influence. We have some in our seminary.

I asked two of them, "What do you remember most about her?"

They said, "She is the most unforgettable person we've ever met. She's still going hard; fills her car with kids and brings them to church."*

Awesome! Yes, this kind of a life is a challenge to all of us. Too many Christians assume that they are in a red-light situation waiting for the light to turn green . . . let's assume, instead that we are at a green light waiting for the red light! It's a matter of perspective and how serious we are about making what we have left in our life count.

Let's combine that challenge with this: Look again at the name of God. Two-thirds of His name is "GO" and if that is turned around, by the same thinking, two-thirds of God's name is "DO"! Therefore the "gospel" is go and do it! Let's put the go and the do into our living. Words aren't enough. Praying isn't enough. It's a balance of doing and going with the message and lifestyle. And people are not very interested in what we say, anyway. People want to see this gospel message, if it's so good, put into an action that can be interpreted as living it out! Go and do . . . NOW!

*Howard Hendricks, *Say It with Love* (Wheaton, IL: Victor Books, 1989).

Today's Quote: *Fear not that your life shall come to an end, but rather that it shall never have a beginning.* — Cardinal Newman

Today's Verse: He said to them, "Go into all the world and preach the good news to all creation" (Mark 16:15).

Day 11
One Tiny Voice

This is the story of a man whom perhaps you have never heard about. He was Telemachus, a fourth-century Christian monk.

He lived in a remote village in Italy, tending his garden, sharing his goods, giving his produce to others, and spending much time in prayer. One day he thought that he had heard the voice of God, or at least a strong impression that he should go to the city of Rome. He immediately obeyed, made his preparations and set out on foot. Some weary weeks later he arrived in the city at the time of one of the great festivals. Telemachus, not knowing what to do, followed the ever-increasing crowd surging down the streets and converging at the Colosseum. He watched as the gladiators stood before the Emperor saying, "We who are about to die salute you." THEN he realized these men were about to fight to the death for the entertainment of the raucous crowd that day. Telemachus shouted, "In the name of Christ, STOP!"

Nobody heard, nor did the ones near him respond. The games began, the gladiators were locked in battle. The monk pushed his way through the shouting crowd, climbed over the wall, and dropped to the dusty floor of the arena. The crowd watched in fascination as this tiny figure ran toward the gladiators, shouting, "In the name of Christ, STOP!" The crowd thought it was part of the entertainment.

The little monk continued until he was right in the middle of the gladiators who had also stopped to watch this interruption. Suddenly the crowd realized it wasn't part of the show and their laughter turned to anger and shouting. As Telemachus was pleading with the gladiators to stop, he turned to the emperor to plead for this carnage to end. One of the gladiators plunged a sword into his body. He dropped to the sand. As he lay bleeding and dying, his last words were: "In the name of Christ, STOP!" The crowd was hushed, they all heard his dying plea.

Then a strange thing happened. As the gladiators looked down at the tiny, bleeding figure in the sand, the crowd was gripped by the drama. Way up in one of the upper rows, one man stood and slowly began to make his way toward the exit. Others followed his lead. And soon, in hushed, deathly silence, everyone left the Colosseum.

That year was 391 B.C. and that was the last battle to the death ever fought in the Roman Colosseum. It changed the thinking of society.

It happened because of one small voice . . . barely heard above the clamor and shouting. Only one voice . . . one unknown, a nobody . . . one life who was willing to speak the truth in the name of God!

Today's Quote: *Courage is fear that has said its prayers.* — Eleanor Doan

Today's Verse: Be strong and very courageous. Be careful to obey all the law my servant Moses gave you; do not turn from it to the right or to the left (Josh. 1:7).

Day 12
The Gnarled Old Oak Tree

One day the woodcutter took his grandson into the forest for his first experience in selecting and cutting oak trees, which they would later sell to the boat builders. As they walked, the woodcutter explained that the purpose of each tree is contained in its natural shape: some are straight for planks, some have the proper curves for the ribs, and some are tall for masts. The woodcutter told his grandson that by paying attention to the details, and with experience recognizing these characteristics, someday he might become the woodcutter of the forest.

A little way into the forest the grandson saw an old oak tree that had never been cut. The boy asked his grandfather if he could cut it down because it was useless for boat building . . . there were no straight limbs, the trunk was short and gnarled, and the curves were going the wrong way. "We could cut it down for firewood," the grandson said, "at least then it will be of some use to us."

The woodcutter replied that for now they should be about their work cutting the proper trees for the boat builders; maybe later they could return to the old oak tree.

After a few hours of cutting the huge trees the grandson grew tired and asked if they could stop for a rest in some cool shade. The woodcutter took his grandson over to the old oak tree, where they rested against its trunk in the cool shade beneath its twisted limbs.

After they had rested a while, the woodcutter explained to his grandson the necessity of attentive awareness and recognition of everything in the forest and in the world. Some things are readily apparent, like the tall, straight trees; other things are less apparent, requiring closer attention, like recognition of the proper curves in the limbs. And some things might initially appear to have no purpose at all, like the gnarled old oak tree.

The woodcutter stated, "You must learn to pay careful attention every day so you can recognize and discover the purpose God has for everything in creation. For it is this old oak tree, which you so quickly deemed useless except for firewood, that now allows us to rest against its trunk amidst the coolness of its shade."

"Remember, my grandson, not everything is as it first appears. Be patient, pay attention, recognize, and discover."*

What great life lessons are in this simple story. But who will have the patience and time to teach these to the young? To the grandchildren? To the next generation? Grandparents who might have the time, patience, attention, recognition, and have already made the discovery?

*Brian Cavanaugh, *The Sower's Seed* (New York, NY: Paulist Press, 1990).

Today's Quote: *One of the most influential handclasps is that of a grandparent around the hand of a grandchild.*

Today's Verse: No good tree bears bad fruit, nor does a bad tree bear good fruit. Each tree is recognized by its own fruit . . . (Luke 6:43–44).

Day 13
We Can't Come Back

Life is full of uncertainties, isn't it? Would any of us argue that point? As humans, we understand that death is perhaps the most uncertain thing that can happen to us. We fear it, wonder at it, explore its mysteries. In the end, we hope to have wisdom and a readiness as death approaches.

A little friend of mine once reminded me of the necessity of accepting death. One day, shortly after the sudden passing of his beloved grandfather, this little fellow, not much past three, gazed out the window of his grandmother's car. They were headed to her house — the same house that had always belonged to her and grandpa.

"Grandma," he said softly, his eyes never leaving the window, "I've been thinking about Grandpa."

"Oh . . . and what were you thinking?"

"Momma said he died and now he lives in heaven with Jesus."

"That's right, sweetheart. Grandpa is in heaven with Jesus."

The little lad then turned away from the window and finished with, "It's too bad we couldn't all go together." Grandma couldn't say anything, as she was fighting back the tears. There was a long pause and then Jordan finished with, "But then we couldn't come back."

I can't be certain about you, but I'm not ashamed to say that story brings a tear to my eye. And a valuable lesson to my mind: God longs

to have a place in eternity for each one of us, but it's up to us to make sure we know the path, and the finality of our choices.

Jesus came to the world as a perfect sacrifice for the human race. He served as our window of escape from a deserved and total punishment.

Death will reach me, and you, and everyone. We need to stop and think about our destination, because, to paraphrase a wise friend of mine: "We can't come back." The day will come when, as Jordan was hoping, we will indeed all go together, when Christ returns for His flock.

How about you, fellow traveler? Are you prepared to learn that supreme lesson about the road we all travel?

Today's Quote: *I alone am responsible for the wrong I do.* — Oswald Chambers

Today's Verse: Then we which are alive and remain shall be caught up together with them in the clouds, to meet the Lord in the air; and so shall we ever be with the Lord (1 Thess. 4:17).

Day 14
But I Am Only . . .

Have you been guilty of hiding behind the excuse, "I am only a senior citizen," or "I am only one person," or "I am only a one-talent person," or "I am only me"? It's a human tendency to excuse our inactivity or lack of action. Well let's take a closer look at this subject.

A couple of years ago the *Wall Street Journal* carried the interesting story about Harry Lipsig, 88 years young, who at that age decided to begin a new law firm. He had worked for over 60 years in a New York law firm helping build their clientele, now he was going to start a whole new firm by himself. The first case accepted was unusual . . . here it is:

A lady was bringing suit against the city of New York because a police officer was driving while drunk in a squad car which struck and killed her 71-year-old husband. Her argument was that the city had deprived her of her husband's future earnings potential. The city countered back with their argument that at age 71, he had little or no earnings potential. They thought they had a clever defense . . . UNTIL it dawned on them that this lady's argument was being advanced by a vigorous 88-year-old attorney! The city of New York settled out of court for $1.25 million! Even our attitudes are the result of choices we make. We can still be a senior in age, but making a difference in life.

Talking about choice. . . . Back when the Romans were the top world power, there was one Roman general who had a unique way in which he dealt with condemned spies who had been caught and brought to trial. Once condemned by trial, he offered the prisoner a choice: The execution squad, or the "Black Door."

It happened again, the spy had been caught, tried in his courtroom and stood before the General as a condemned spy. The General asked, "What will you choose, the execution squad or the black door?" The man's choice was the execution squad.

He was led away and the sounds of the judgment carried back into the room where the general and his aide are sitting. "General," the aide asked, "what is behind the black door?"

"Freedom," the General replied, "but few men have the courage to choose the unknown, even over death."

Let's make our attitudinal choice. No longer will we say, "I am only . . . ." Instead we will choose freedom, choose to be involved, choose to make a difference. The bottom line is that an attitude of "I am only" is not pleasing to God. Please note our verse for today!

Today's Quote: *You are no longer a human being, you are now a human becoming.*

Today's Verse: The Lord said to me, "Do not say, 'I am only a child.' You must go to everyone I send you to and say whatever I command you. Do not be afraid of them, for I am with you and will rescue you" (Jer. 1:7–8).

Some Retirement Definitions

Sixty-five is the age when one acquires sufficient experience to lose his/her job.

There are a lot of books telling you how to manage when you retire. Most people want one that'll tell them how to manage in the meantime.

Retirement can be a great joy if you can figure how to spend time without spending any money.

Forty years ago when a person said something about retiring, they were usually talking about going to bed.

Today, "retirement security" is making sure all the doors are locked before you go to bed.

One wife's definition of retirement: "Twice as much husband and only half as much income."

Mandatory retirement is another form of compulsory poverty.

Retirement has cured many a businessman's ulcers . . . and given his wife one!

And now let's read a tidbit from the life of Carl Johnson of Kankakee, Illinois: My wife and I took our grandchildren to visit my parents in Missouri. When we were ready to leave, my dad gave me a picture of myself. I had sent it to my parents during the Second World War. I was dressed in my complete army uniform on which I had pinned my medals. As I walked out the door and into the yard, Amy, my five-year-old granddaughter, asked, "Who is that? Papa, is that you?"

I answered, "Yes, that is a picture of me."

Then she asked, "Did you you fight in the war?"

I replied, "Yes, I fought in the war."

When we arrived home, my daughter and son-in-law came to get the children. Amy was still excited, she could hardly wait to tell her parents about her war hero. She grabbed the picture and ran to her mother. Excitedly, she said, "Mother, I think I know something you don't know. Did you know that Papa fought in the Civil War?"*

What is the bottom line? Too many seniors have been taught to study, know, proclaim, and practice the Word of God. Yet there are still people who think seniors are only scarred, cracked, chipped, crumbled, and broken antiques of no value. Therefore they are set aside.

Don't let anyone put you down because you're a senior! You have great value, you still have much to contribute . . . especially to grandkids and their parents.

*Carl Johnson, *Parables, Etc.,* 7/91.

Today's Quote: *Success seems to be largely a matter of hanging on after others have let go.* — System Forms Brochure

Today's Verse: The righteous will flourish like a palm tree. . . .they will still bear fruit in old age, they will stay fresh and green, proclaiming, "The Lord is upright; He is my Rock . . ." (Ps. 92:12–15).

Even God Can't Get In

There was a little, old cleaning lady, humble, clean, but she had to live on the "wrong side of the tracks" because of her meager earnings. She attempted to become a member at the fashionable "First" church. The pastor was not eager to have a seedy-looking lady in faded, out-of-style clothing sitting next to any of his wealthy, up-town members.

Her efforts at attempting to join this church had gone on for over a year . . . but she was persistent. So she called again, the seventh time, to set an appointment to discuss membership and her joining. The pastor put her off once more.

"I'll tell you what to do," the pastor said in his most pious-sounding voice. "You just go home tonight and have a talk with God about it. Really pray about it. Then, later, you can tell me what God said to you about your membership in our church."

Weeks went by until they became months. He saw no more of her. No more attempts to set an appointment. He did allow as to the fact that his conscience bothered him a little. Then one day as he was on his way to an appointment downtown, he noticed her. Here she was in her uniform, scrubbing the floors in the foyer of this office building.

He stopped when he recognized her and felt that he should at least ask. "Did you ever have your little talk with God about church membership, Mrs. Pettibone?"

"Oh, my, yes," she replied, "I talked with God just as you suggested."

"Ah . . . and just what did He tell you?"

"Well, Preacher," she paused, brushed away a couple of wisps of hair with her work-worn hand, put her hands on her hips and replied, "God told me not to be discouraged, but simply to keep on trying for my membership. He also said that He himself has been trying, without success, to get into your church for more than 20 years!"

Oh . . . oh, big trouble in River City! Honesty with a punch! Wow! What about your church? Is God on the outside looking in? Maybe, even more importantly, what about you and your life? Is God at home on the inside or is He still standing outside and seeking entrance?

It's so easy to fill our lives with the urgent and forget about the really important! We get so busy doing "religious things," "churchy things," but where is the Lord in all of our busyness? Outside, or on the inside? Too many of us like to keep God in a Sunday-kind-of-box. It's nice to go to His House . . . but to take Him home with us may be a bit too close for comfort. His presence may cramp our style.

Today's Quote: *If God did not exist, it would be necessary to invent Him.* — Voltaire

Today's Verse: Here I am! I stand at the door and knock. If anyone hears my voice and opens the door, I will come in . . . (Rev. 3:20).

The Beggar King

Once there was a time, according to legend, when Ireland was ruled by a king who had no sons, no grandsons, no heirs. The king sent out his couriers to post notices in all the towns of his realm. The notices advised that every qualified young man should apply for an interview with the king as a possible successor to the throne. However, all such candidates must have these two qualifications: 1) they must love God and 2) love fellow human beings.

The young man about whom this legend centers saw a notice and reflected that he loved God and also his neighbors. One thing stopped him . . . he was so poor that he had no clothes that would be presentable in the sight of the king. Neither could he purchase the provisions needed for the long journey to the castle. So the young man begged here and borrowed there and worked at odd jobs until he managed enough for appropriate clothes and some provisions for the journey.

Properly attired, the young man set out on his journey and had almost finished the trip when he came upon a poor beggar by the roadside. The beggar was dressed in tattered rags, and he pleaded for help, "I'm hungry and I'm cold. Please, please help me . . . please?"

The young man was so touched by the beggar's plight that he immediately took off his new clothes and exchanged them with the tattered rags of the beggar. Without any kind of hesitation, he also gave him all the provisions he had left.

Now, somewhat hesitant, he continued on his way to the castle dressed in the rags of the beggar and no provisions for his walk back home. When he arrived, one of the king's attendants met him in the great hall. After a brief break to clean off some of the grime from the trip, he was finally admitted to the throne room where the king sat.

The young man bowed in reverence. When he looked up, he gasped in astonishment. "You . . . it's you! You are the beggar by the road."

"Yes," the king replied with a smile, "I was that beggar."

"But . . . bu . . . you aren't a beggar. You are the real king! Why?" he managed to stammer out after gaining some of his composure.

"Because I had to find out if you or any of the other young men really loved God and your fellow human beings," replied the king. "If we met as we are now, I would never really know if you cared enough about others. So I used this ploy. I have discovered that you do really, sincerely love God and others. You will be the next king, you will be my successor. You will inherit this kingdom!"

Today's Quote: *How shall we become lovely? By loving Him who is ever lovely.* — St. Augustine

Today's Verse: A new command I give you: Love one another. As I have loved you, so you must love one another. By this all men will know that you are my disciples, if you love one another (John 13:34–35).

To Feed the Birds

About 20 years ago, Los Angeles residents were shocked and saddened to learn that one of their own was starving himself just to be able to feed the birds in two different city parks. Newspaper reporters learned of the strange story and reported it nationally. Retired Raymond Lopez, 80, gaunt, sick, and feeble, explained, "I don't care about myself anymore. I'm only interested in helping all things that suffer and all things that are hungry."

Most of Lopez's social security check and small pension went to pay the delivery man who came every Tuesday with 2,000 pounds of feed for his fine-feathered friends. The bill came to about $150 per week. Many of his friends had encouraged Lopez to take a trip, to relax, or to enjoy other material things of this life. To such suggestions he merely replied, "I'd rather go hungry myself than let my birds go hungry."

A good many of us would question the wisdom of the bird lover's actions. Still, the elderly Californian has learned one of the more valuable lessons of life. I believe he discovered that it is more blessed to give than to receive.

This world seems to be divided into two camps of people — the givers and getters. We could also call them the eternalist and the materialist. Jesus dealt a lot with these two philosophies of life and firmly positioned himself on the side of the givers.

The taker, the getter, is one who believes he/she must take all, even from the weak and helpless. This person fares quite well until another comes along who is stronger and takes what the getter has been taking. Some have labeled this concept as "the survival of the fittest." It's part of Darwin's theory of life.

Take the giver — this eternalist believes in ultimate accountability before God and knows he is placed on earth not as a taker but as one who is called upon to help, to give, to love, and be a positive influence for good. Most of the world laughs at the giver. Still, this is the only person who really endures. This person has placed treasures where earth's fickle circumstances cannot touch them.

It is important that we find a cause to live with and for, that is larger than who we are. Let Mr. Lopez of bird-lover note be a challenge to all of us as we live. Are you a getter or a giver?

Today's Quote: *He who shall introduce into public affairs the principles of primitive Christianity will change the face of the world!* — Benjamin Franklin

Today's Verse: Seek ye first the kindom of God, and His righteousness; and all these things shall be added unto you (Matt. 6:33;KJV).

Day 19
Hope Beyond

At the age of 80, the well-known poet Alfred Lord Tennyson was being taken from his summer home at Aldworth, England, to his winter residence on the Isle of Wight. As the boat left the mainland and crossed the strait, Tennyson heard a moaning sound caused by the fierce beating of the waves against a large sandbar. He recognized this as a prelude to a coming storm.

A few days later, his health began to fail and a nurse was hired to stay with him. In conversing with him, she said quietly, "Sir, you've composed a great many poems, but few hymns. I wish you'd write one now on your sick bed. I'm sure it would help and comfort other poor sufferers."

The next morning, Tennyson handed her a scrap of paper, saying, "I followed your suggestion and wrote these verses during the night."

The poem/hymn proved to be a masterpiece filled with imagery about the sea, the emotions related to dying which the "moaning of the bar" brought to his mind and the glorious hope of seeing Jesus at the end of life's voyage. The selection reads in part:

Sunset and evening star, and one clear call for me!
And may there be no moaning of the bar, when I put out to
    sea.
Twilight and evening bell, and after that the dark!

And may there be no sadness of farewell, when I embark.
For though from out the bourne of time and place the flood
    may bear me far,
I hope to see my Pilot face to face when I have crossed the
    bar!

There will come the time for all of us to cross the bar! It's a whole lot sooner today that it has been at any time in our past. When you become a grandparent, you begin to think about how this life is going to end. We have observed the cycles of life . . . birth and death . . . young and then old . . . in fact, we have lived through many of these life cycles. It's time to think about going home, running the last lap, finishing the race, putting the final AMEN to this life.

Will death be your enemy or your friend? The answer to that all depends upon how you have lived your life to this moment. If you, my friend, have never made a decision to make the Lord Jesus Christ your Saviour, this can be your moment. With your confession, you can invite Him to be your Guide, your "Pilot" as Tennyson put it, into and through all of eternity. It's a choice that only you can make.

Today's Quote: *We are saved by a Person, and only by a Person, and only by one Person.* — William F. McDowell

Today's Verse: For the wages of sin is death, but the gift of God is eternal life in Christ Jesus our Lord (Rom. 6:23).

Joy and Laughter

Can you remember a time when your life was more joyful? I can! A recent study found that kids laugh an average of 150 times a day while adults laugh only about 10 times a day! What's happened to us? We have a laughter famine . . . especially in the church. We need to laugh at ourselves and with others.

John Updike, contemporary American novelist, describes his parents as "inclined to laugh a lot, and examine everything for the fingerprints of God!"

Laughter is one of those good gifts from God! Most of us tend to live deadpan. We tackle every problem head-on without the release of laughter!

Grandmother and granddaughter, a precocious 10 year old, were spending the evening together when the little girl suddenly looked up and asked, "How old are you, Grandma?"

The woman was a bit startled, but knowing her granddaughter's quick little mind, she wasn't too shocked. "Well, honey, when you're my age you don't share your age with anybody."

"Aw, go ahead, Grandma . . . you can trust me!"

"No dear, I never tell anyone my age."

Grandma got busy fixing dinner and suddenly realized the little darling had been absent for about 20 minutes . . . much too long! She checked and found her upstairs in her bedroom. Her granddaughter had dumped the contents of her purse on top of her bed and was sitting in the middle of the mess, holding her grandmother's driver's license.

When their eyes met, the child announced, "Grandma, you're 76!"

"Why, yes, I am. How did you know that?"

"I found the date of your birthday here on your driver's license and subtracted that year from this year . . . so you're 76!"

"That's right, sweetheart. Your grandmother is 76."

The little girl continued staring at the driver's license and added, "You also made an 'F' in sex, Grandma!"*

Somewhere between childhood innocence and NOW, life has become too grim! When did a well-exercised sense of humor and joy get sacrificed on the altar of adulthood? Who says that being a Christian means you must have a long face? To be joyful is a choice! To laugh is a choice! Let's choose to laugh and be joyful!

*James S. Huett, *Illustrations Unlimited* (Wheaton, IL: Tyndale House Publishers, 1988).

Today's Quote: *Although it is a far cry from there to here, he laughed all the way.* — Arthur "Bugs" Baer

Today's Verse: Though the fig tree does not bud and there are no grapes on the vines, though the olive crop fails and the field produce no food, though there are no sheep in the pen and no cattle in the stalls, yet I will rejoice in the Lord, I will be joyful in God my Savior (Hab. 3:17–18).

Natural Instincts

Two brothers wished very much to receive a generous inheritance from their aged grandfather. Both spent many, many hours tending to his every whim in order to gain his favor and have the inside track. They would gladly wash his car inside and out, clean his house, mow the yard, fix his meals, run his errands, and do his shopping.

One day, the old man, a bit weary of the whole thing, asked them a question: "Is a child born well-mannered and considerate, or is it something that one must be taught?" As chance would have it, each brother took one side of the argument, hoping that would be the opinion of their grandfather. The two brothers began to argue and debate . . . this went on for days, loudly and insistent. Finally, their grandfather said, "Bring me proof to back up your argument. One year from today, I will give the larger inheritance to the one of you who can bring me positive proof to back up your point of view on this issue."

One year later to the day, the two brothers returned. Both claimed to have proof. The first brother barked out this command: "Please bring my dear grandfather a cup of coffee." To the amazement of the elderly gentleman, a cat wearing a tiny apron walked in from the kitchen carrying a steaming cup of coffee, a creamer, and sugar on a silver tray. The cat was something else. This brother had trained the cat to walk on hind legs and balance the tray with the front paws. After placing the tray on the coffee table, this cat bowed low and stood at full attention.

The grandfather said, "Never have I seen anything like that!" The implications were so obvious. . . . "If you can train a cat like that, then a person can be trained to behave respectfully," continued the grandfather. He was about to promise this grandson a huge inheritance.

"Just wait a moment, Grandpa," protested the other brother, "you have not given me my opportunity to present my proof." This brother had been aware of the extraordinary cat his brother had trained and for months he was in deep despair fearing he would lose his inheritance to a trained cat. What should he do? On this day he was ready. From his pocket he produced a small box and said, "Here is the proof that one cannot change the way one is born." With a flourish, he placed the box on the floor and opened the lid. Out popped one small mouse which scampered across the floor in front of the cat! The cat forgot all his training, and still dressed in the small apron followed in hot pursuit!

At the moment of crisis, natural instincts surfaced . . . the cat was not a trained butler. It was still a cat. What it needed was a new nature!

Today's Quote: *Better never to have been born at all than never to have been born again.* — Eleanor Doan

Today's Verse: Jesus declared, "I tell you the truth, no one can see the kingdom of God unless he is born again" (John 3:3).

Day 22
Surprise Purchase

The very wealthy English Baron Fitzgerald had only one child, a son, who understandably was the apple of his eye, the center of his affections, the focus of this little family's attention.

The son grew up, but in his early teens his mother died, leaving him and his father. Fitzgerald grieved over the loss of his wife but devoted himself to fathering their son. In the passing of time, the son became very ill and died in his late teens. In the meantime, the Fitzgerald financial holdings greatly increased. The father had used much of his wealth to acquire art works of the "masters."

With the passing of more time, Fitzgerald himself became ill and died. Previous to his death he had carefully prepared his will with explicit instructions as to how his estate would be settled. He had directed that there would be an auction in which his entire art collection would be sold. Because of the quantity and quality of the art works in his collection which was valued in the the millions of English pounds, a huge crowd of prospective buyers had gathered, expectantly. Among them were many museum curators and private collectors eager to bid. The art works were displayed for viewing before the auction began. Among them was one painting which received very little attention. It was of poor quality and done by an unknown local artist. It happened to be a portrait of Fitzgerald's only son.

When the time came for the auction to begin, the auctioneer gaveled the crowd to attention and before the bidding began, the attorney read first from the will of Fitzgerald which instructed that the first painting to be auctioned was the painting of "my beloved son."

The poor quality painting didn't receive any bidders . . . except one! The only bidder was the old servant who had known the son and loved him and served him, and for sentimental reasons offered the only bid. For less than an English pound he bought the painting.

The auctioneer stopped the bidding and asked the attorney to read again from the will. The crowd was hushed, it was quite unusual, and the attorney read from the Fitzgerald will: "Whoever buys my son gets all my art collection. The auction is over!"

Whoever gets the son gets it all! Whoever gets Jesus, God's only Son, gets it all! It's that simple and that important. If you don't have the Son of God as part of your life, you really have nothing in the end! If you have the Son, you have all that God has to offer! All this and heaven, too! Whoever gets the Son gets it all!

Today's Quote: *You will never know that Jesus is all you need until Jesus is all you've got.* — Mother Teresa

Today's Verse: And this is the testimony: God has given us eternal life, and this life is in His Son. He who has the Son has life; he who does not have the Son of God does not have life (1 John 5:11–12).

Day 23
The Failure

For more than 20 years Robert Frost was a failure. He was considered a failure by friends, neighbors, and publishers. It was a lonely, frustrating struggle for recognition and publication which never seemed willing to come his way. He often said that during this time of struggle he was one of the few persons who knew he was a poet.

The world has since mourned his passing and today he towers as one of America's greatest writers of verse. His poems have been published in 22 different languages at last count. The American edition of his poems has sold more than a million copies.

Frost was a four-time winner of the coveted Pulitzer Prize for poetry and had more honorary degrees thrust on him than any other man of letters. He was in constant demand to read his writings.

Robert Frost was 39 before he was able to sell his first volume of poetry to any publisher. He had been writing for more than 20 years before he was accepted to be published. His writing for those long years met with an endless stream of rejection slips, yet he kept on writing and submitting his work. Finally his perseverance paid off. He was published and considered a poet. Today we can say that the world is a bit wiser and richer for the writings of Robert Frost.

An eminent psychiatrist, Dr. George Crane, recently listed various ingredients necessary for greatness. Among those qualities he noted are some you'd expect to find — talent, responsibility, etc. Then, surprisingly, he said that physical stamina is also necessary! He reasons that many men do not reach the apex of their life endeavors until quite late in life and therefore endurance is necessary. He cited Winston Churchill as a prime example.

What is true in the physical realm of life is also true in the spiritual part of living. If we are to reach the ultimate in what God wants us to be, there must be spiritual endurance. This quality is called "longsuffering" as well as "patience" in the Bible. The apostle Paul even lists longsuffering as a fruit of the Spirit.

In this struggle it's the little things that drive us to despair. You can sit on a mountain, but not on a tack. To reach your goal in life will take endurance, but it's worth the struggle. Hang in there!

Today's Quote: *The battle against evil is difficult, not so much because of the action required, but because of the endurance necessary to achieve victory!* — Eleanor L. Doan

Today's Verse: But he that shall endure unto the end, the same shall be saved (Mark 13:13;KJV).

Does It Pay?

Max Jukes lived in the state of New York. He was not a Christian and did not believe in any sort of Christian training. His was the life of a reprobate. The girl he married was of the same opinion and had the same sort of questionable character. These were not nice people by any stretch of the imagination. Their personal lives and their home life was a mess.

Out of this union they have 1,026 descendants. Each of these descendants were followed through their lifetime with these results:

Three hundred of them died prematurely. One hundred of these descendants were sentenced to spend an average of 13 years each in prisons. One hundred-ninety of the girls were public prostitutes. There were more than 100 drunkards.

The results are that this family of descendants ended up costing the state and federal government millions of dollars — dollars that were spent to care for them on the welfare rolls, as well as making room for them in the prisons — and let alone what they cost in their immoral influence. Not a one of these descendants made any kind of a positive contribution to society that could be found.

But . . .

Jonathan Edwards lived in the same state at about the same time. He believed in Christian training. He was a well-known preacher in his day. He lived his religion in his home life. The girl he married also was a committed Christian and set about to raise their family in these same concepts.

From this union they had 729 descendants that were studied. Out of this family have come 300 preachers. Further, 65 went on to become college professors and 13 became college presidents. Sixty of these family members became authors of what would be considered good books with a positive influence. Three were elected to become United States congressmen, and one was elected vice-president of the United States.

And except for Aaron Burr, a grandson of Edwards who married a lady of questionable character, the family has not cost the state or federal government a single dollar to care for. The Edwards family was a family who impacted our nation in a very positive way.

What's the major difference? Christian commitment and training against the absence of such. We must also add that the vast majority of the Edwards family became Christians at an early age.

Today's Quote: *A child educated only at school is an uneducated child.* — Santayana

Today's Verse: Train a child in the way he should go, and when he is old he will not turn from it (Prov. 22:6;NIV).

Just an Ordinary Woman

Rosa Parks is just a very ordinary woman, a seamstress in an Alabama department store. On December 1, 1955, she made history! She boarded her usual bus for the ride home after work. It so happened that the "black" section in the back of the bus was full. The center section was available to blacks as long as no whites needed those seats. Rosa took the lone remaining seat of the center section. The bus continued . . . three stops later some whites were picked up, just enough to fill each remaining seat with one white man still standing. The bus driver informed Parks and three other black riders that they must vacate the center section so this white man could take his "rightful" seat.

Parks tells us in her own words what happened next: "When the driver first spoke, didn't any of us move; but then he spoke a second time with what I call a threat, because he said, 'Ya'll better make it light on yourselves and let me have those seats.' At that point the other three stood up . . . the driver looked at me and asked me if I was going to stand up. I told him, 'No, I wasn't.' He said, 'If you don't stand up, I'm going to have you arrested.' I told him to go on and have me arrested. He didn't exchange any more words with me."

Rosa was arrested and spent the night in the Montgomery jail. Forty of the pastors of Montgomery churches pledged to lead a boycott of the city bus service until segregation would no longer be the practice. A new young pastor among the 40, Martin Luther King Jr., was selected to lead the boycott. Rosa was convicted in court and fined $14 for violating the laws of segregation. It was appealed to the U.S. Supreme Court which overturned this lower court decision. This was the moment when a lethal blow was struck which toppled all segregation laws and what had been any legal foundations justifying such laws.

Later, then Governor Jay S. Hammond of Alaska declared May 23, 1982, as "Rosa Parks Day" in honor of this courageous, ordinary woman who made a difference for human rights for all of God's people. On this day in Alaska, she had come in contact with laryngitis and couldn't talk. So her friend Ashley Dickerson introduced her to the crowd gathered to hear this 69-year-old lady speak with these words: "Rosa, you don't have to say anything. Your life has spoken!"

Powerful words: Your life has spoken! Here's a very ordinary lady, by her own description, who was willing to take a stand and be counted. She became the catalyst in a very extraordinary way to make life better for a whole lot of God's people everywhere.

Today's Quote: *When opportunity knocks, let it in and offer it a chair!*

Today's Verse: For if you remain silent at this time, relief and deliverance for the Jews will arise from another place, but you and your father's family will perish. And who knows but that you have come to royal position for such a time as this? (Esther 4:14).

Day 26
Remember the Duck?

While a little boy was visiting with his grandparents, his grandfather helped him make his first slingshot. It was a beautiful weapon, and he had great fun playing with it in the woods. He would take aim and let the stone fly, but he never hit a thing.

Then, on his way home for lunch, the little boy cut through the backyard and saw one of Grandmother's pet ducks. He took aim at the moving target and let the stone fly. Lo and behold, it went straight to the mark and hit the duck in the head, instantly killing it! Talk about a lucky shot, a one in a million!

The boy panicked. In frightened desperation he picked up the dead duck and hid it in the nearby woodpile. At that instant, he saw his sister Sally standing over by the corner of the house. She had seen the whole thing. They went into eat, but Sally said nothing.

After lunch was over, Grandmother said, "Okay, Sally, let's clear the table and wash the dishes."

Sally said, "Oh, Grandmother, Johnny said he wanted to help you in the kitchen today. Didn't you, Johnny?" And then she whispered to him, "Remember the duck!"

So Johnny helped with the dishes. Later in the day, Grandfather called the children to go fishing. Grandmother said, "I'm sorry, but Sally can't go. She has to stay here and help me clean the house and get supper."

Sally smiled and said, "That's all been taken care of. Johnny said he wanted to help today, didn't you Johnny?" And then she whispered, "Remember the duck!"

Now this went on for several days. Johnny did all the chores — his and those assigned to Sally. Finally, he could stand it no longer, so he went to his grandmother and confessed it all.

His grandmother took him in her arms and said, "I know, Johnny. I was standing at the kitchen window, and I saw the whole thing. And because I love you, I forgave you. I wondered just how long you would let Sally make a slave of you by using your guilt against you. Didn't you know that I love you and would always forgive you?"

That night Sally again tried her tactic. She volunteered Johnny with her whispered threat, "Remember the duck!"

This time Johnny almost shouted it out loud, "That won't work on me anymore. Grandma knows all about it, and I'm free!"

Jesus Christ came to set us free from our guilt and shame. With one simple confession of our sin, we can receive God's forgiveness.

Today's Quote: *Guilt always makes for cowards!* — Unknown

Today's Verse: But if we walk in the light, as he is in the light, we have fellowship with one another, and the blood of Jesus, his Son, purifies us from all sin (1 John 1:7).

Day 27
Black Pebble? White Pebble?

Many years ago, when people who owed money could be thrown into jail, a merchant in Rome had the misfortune to owe a huge sum of money to a mean moneylender. The moneylender, who was quite old and ugly, took a fancy to the merchant's beautiful young granddaughter, whom they had been raising because her parents had died. The moneylender proposed a bargain. He would cancel the merchant's debt if he could have the granddaughter instead and make her his wife.

Both the merchant and the granddaughter were horrified at the bargain, so the cunning moneylender schemed that they would let "Providence" decide the matter. He told them that he would put a black pebble and a white pebble into an empty bag and the granddaughter would have to pick out one of the pebbles. If she picked the black one, she would become his wife, and her grandfather's debt would be canceled. If she refused to pick a pebble, her grandfather would be thrown into jail and eventually she would starve with no one to care for her.

Reluctantly, the merchant-grandfather agreed. They were standing on a pebble strewn path in the merchant's garden as they talked. The moneylender stooped down to pick up the two pebbles. As he did, the girl, senses heightened by fright, sharp-eyed, noticed that he picked up two black pebbles and put them into the bag. The money lender then asked the girl to pick out the pebble that would decide her fate and that of her grandfather.

What would you have done if you were the girl? If you had to advise her, what would you have advised her to do?

1) The girl should refuse to pick a pebble?

2) The girl should show that there are two black pebbles in the bag and expose the moneylender as a cheat?

3) The girl should pick the black pebble and sacrifice herself in order to spare her grandfather from prison?

The girl put her hand into the bag and drew out a pebble. But, without looking at it, she fumbled it and let the pebble fall onto the path where it was immediately mixed in among all the other pebbles. "Oh, how clumsy of me," she said. "Never mind, however. If you look into the bag, you'll be able to tell which pebble I dropped by the color of the one that remains."

Since the remaining pebble, was, of course, black, it had to be assumed that she had picked the white pebble. Then, for sure, the moneylender dared not admit his own dishonesty!

Today's Quote: *Oftimes the test of courage becomes rather to live than to die.* — Vittorio Alfieri

Today's Verse: I am sending you out like sheep among wolves. Therefore be as shrewd as snakes and as innocent as doves (Matt. 10:16).

Day 28
It's All in Your Attitude

Extravagances and luxuries did not exist for my mother. The one exception to her frugality was a frilly nightgown which she had never worn. She explained, "I have that nightgown so that if I ever have to go to the hospital, I'll still look nice."

Many years later, my mother began to suffer from a mysterious disease which destroyed her health and vitality. On a winter day just before her 69th birthday, she packed up her nightgown and checked into the hospital for tests.

The physician confided with me over the final test results. My mother had only a matter of weeks to live. I agonized for days over whether to tell her the news. Was there any hope I could give her?

I decided not to tell her . . . not just yet. I resolved instead to lift her spirits on her birthday by giving her the most expensive and beautiful matching nightgown and robe I could find. At the very least she would feel like the prettiest person in the hospital, dignified as she lay dying.

After unwrapping the present, my mother said nothing. Finally, pointing to the unwrapped package on her bed, she asked, "Would you mind returning it to the store? I don't really want it." She then picked up a newspaper and pointing to an ad for a summertime designer purse, she explained, "This is what I really want." Why would my ever-frugal mother want an expensive summer purse in the middle of winter, when she couldn't even use it until June?

Then I realized . . . my mother was asking me how long I thought she would live . . . if she would make it to summer. Maybe, if I thought she'd live long enough to use the purse, then she really would. When I brought the purse to her in her hospital bed, she held it tightly against her, with a smile on her face.

Many years later, that particular purse is long worn out, as are half a dozen others. Next week Mother celebrates her 83rd birthday! My gift to her? The most expensive purse I can find. She will use it well!*

Yes . . . it is in attitude! That's not the only reason why we live or die . . . but it effects our living and when we die. One surgeon told me, as I stood by the bedside of his next patient, "I'm glad to see you, Reverend. It really helps my patients to have a support system. The people that pray recover sooner and I've found they live longer than people who don't pray." Now that's not scientific . . . but personal observation from a doctor-surgeon. It's in your attitude!

*Don Shelby sermon, "Where God Can Be Seen," adapted by Jeff Meaney.

Today's Quote: *We don't see things as they are, we see them as we are.* — Anais Nin

Today's Verse: Finally . . . whatever is true, whatever is noble, whatever is right, whatever is pure, whatever is lovely, whatever is admirable . . . if anything is excellent or praiseworthy . . . think about such things (Phil. 4:8).

Day 29
Winding Down

General Douglas MacArthur evaluated his life on his 75th birthday, saying, "Nobody grows old merely by living a number of years. People grow old by deserting their ideals. Years may wrinkle the skin, but to give up interest wrinkles the soul. In the central place of every heart, there is a recording chamber; so long as it receives messages of beauty, hope, cheer, and courage, so long are you young. When the wires are all down and your heart is covered with the snows of pessimism and the ice of cynicism, then are you grown old."

Benjamin Disraeli, former prime minister, expressed it like this in a letter to Lady Bradford: "I am certain there is no greater misfortune than to have a heart that will not grow old. The wisdom of the heart is its growing old in experience, recollected in tranquility, and digested in grace, humility, and love. What other wisdom is worth seeing and having? If people are rightly aging, they are growing in that wisdom, and as their years increase so does this wisdom."

G.K. Chesterton tells us that his old Victorian grandfather grew more silent as he grew older. One day his grown-up sons were complaining about a portion of the "General Thanks-giving" in the *Book of Common Prayer.* It is wicked, they were saying, to thank God for creation when so many people have little reason to be thankful for their miserable existence. The old man broke his silence to say, "I would thank God for my creation if I knew I was a lost soul."

Simcox wrote, "I love people more, because now I can dare let myself love them for their own beauty of being instead of what I can get from them. This change in the focus and the very nature of my loving is a change of the command of myself from eros to agape, from loving others for my sake to loving others for theirs."

William Saroyan said while dying of cancer in his seventies, "I am growing old. I'm falling apart. And I find it VERY INTERESTING when it was most painfully coming apart."

Sir W. Grenfell reportedly wrote this while in his twenties: "As for the life to come, I know nothing about it, but I want it, whatever it is."

Paul the Apostle, in the second letter to the church in Corinth, tells us that nature is winding down, petering out, while the inner self is being renewed. It's this new being which is composed of what remains of the old disintegrating self. Aging beautifully is a decision!

Today's Quote: *For age is opportunity, no less than youth itself, though in another dress, and as the evening twilight fades away the sky is filled with stars, invisible by day.* — Henry Wadsworth Longfellow

Today's Verse: Therefore we do not lose heart. Though outwardly we are wasting away, yet inwardly we are being renewed day by day (2 Cor. 4:16).

Day 30
Life Cycles Go On

An old man and his grandson were spending time together one day. As often happened, the little boy was plying his grandad with questions. Suddenly, with a very serious tone the little boy asked, "Grandfather, what happens when you die?"

The old man explained to the best of his ability, but the boy only looked at him in wonder. "Does that mean you won't be here with me anymore?" the boy asked.

The old man shook his head and said, "Yes, that is true."

"Does that mean you won't be able to play catch with me anymore?" asked the boy.

"Yes," said the old man, "it is true."

"Does it mean you won't be able to fly a kite with me anymore?"

"Yes," said the old man, "it is true."

"Does it mean you won't be able to take me fishing anymore?" asked the boy.

"Yes," said the old man, "it is true."

"Well," said the boy, "who will do those things, if you are not?"

And the old man responded, "My son, when that time comes, it will be time for you to do those things for another little boy."*

Yes, the time will come for the next generation to pass it on. Which brings to mind another thought — what will they have from our generation to pass on to the next? What are we leaving behind which will be important enough to pass on to the next generation?

There is an old parable about a spider who decided one day to move, so he spun a long strand of web in a barn rafter. Then on the next level down he fastened himself to a two-by-four and spun a great web. By and by he died and left this estate to his son, who in turn left it to his son, who in turn left it to his son.

The carefully built structure was a bit antique at this point and the great-grandson spider was walking along one day and tripped over a strand of old web. So he thought, *These are out of style right now and in the way. The first step of up-dating will be to cut this strand.* He then reached over and nipped off what just happened to be the single strand upon which the whole web was hanging and he fell to his death on the barn floor below.

It's a challenge . . . but will our generation pass along life principles that are so important they will not be discarded by the next? Let's keep at it and not give up.

*John D. Gondol, *Responding in Gratitude*.

Today's Quote: *There are two kinds of fools: one says, "This is old, therefore it is good"; the other says, "This is new, therefore it is better."* —William R. Inge

Today's Verse: Train a child in the way he should go, and when he is old he will not turn from it (Prov. 22:6).